A Taste
of culture

Foods of
Iceland

Barbara Sheen

KIDHAVEN PRESS
A part of Gale, Cengage Learning

GALE
CENGAGE Learning™

Detroit • New York • San Francisco • New Haven, Conn • Waterville, Maine • London

LIBRARY OF CONGRESS CATALOGING-IN-PUBLICATION DATA

Sheen, Barbara.
  Foods of Iceland / by Barbara Sheen.
    p. cm. -- (A taste of culture)
  Includes bibliographical references and index.
  ISBN 978-0-7377-5869-6 (hardcover)
  1. Cooking, Icelandic--Juvenile literature. 2. Food--Iceland--Juvenile literature. 3. Iceland--Social life and customs--Juvenile literature. 4. Cookbooks. I. Title.
  TX723.5.I2S54 2011
  641.59417--dc22
                                                                    2011005784

Kidhaven Press
27500 Drake Rd.
Farmington Hills MI 48331

ISBN-13: 978-0-7377-5869-6
ISBN-10: 0-7377-5869-4

Printed in the United States of America
1 2 3 4 5 6 7 15 14 13 12 11

Printed by Bang Printing, Brainerd, MN, 1st Ptg., 05/2011

contents

Pure Healthy Food

Iceland is a unique place. This isolated volcanic island that borders the Arctic Circle is one of the most unspoiled countries on Earth. Despite occasional volcanic activity that releases ash into the air, Iceland has what may be the cleanest air and water and the purest food supply in the world.

Icelandic farmers practice **sustainable farming**. They grow and raise food in a way that preserves the land for future use. They do not use chemicals or pesticides on crops, or feed livestock drugs or growth hormones. Icelandic fishermen also are careful not to pollute the ocean or endanger any species of fish by overfishing. The Icelandic government helps to keep

FOOD REGIONS OF ICELAND

GREENLAND

Greenland Sea

Denmark Strait

Siglufjördhur

Reykjavík

ICELAND

Norwegian Sea

ATLANTIC OCEAN

Faroe Islands

Dairy
Potatoes
Fish
Grains
Cattle
Lamb
Vegetables

the country's food supply pure, too, by enforcing laws that promote the cleanliness of the nation's air, water, and food supply. Icelandic cooks also choose healthful ingredients, such as fish and seafood, lamb, dairy products, and hearty vegetables, that reflect this commitment to purity.

Fish and Seafood

"One half of our fatherlands is the ocean,"[1] an old Icelandic proverb says. To a large degree, the ocean has shaped Iceland's culture. Its first settlers were **Vikings**, famous seafaring explorers, warriors, and pirates who sailed in longships from **Scandinavia** in the 9th century. Ever since then, the North Atlantic Ocean and Iceland's many inland waterways have been an important part of the Icelandic people's lives. Icelandic waters

Fish is plentiful in Iceland and is one of the most common things that Icelanders eat every day.

Renewable Energy

Icelanders' concern for the environment is shown in the fuels they use. Rather than only using fossil fuels that will eventually run out, 81 percent of the energy Icelanders use comes from renewable sources.

Iceland's geography contains many natural energy sources. Iceland has more than twenty steam fields, or geysers, with water that is at least 300° F (150° C). This steam is known as geothermal energy. It heats Icelandic buildings, swimming pools, and even streets, where underground pipes keep sidewalks free of ice.

Iceland's many waterfalls provide another power source called hydropower, or water power. Hydropower is changed to electricity. Combined with geothermal energy, it provides 100 percent of Iceland's electricity.

Hydrogen is another energy source. Currently, Icelandic scientists are working to change all the nation's motor vehicles and its fishing fleet from gas to hydrogen power by 2050.

contain plenty of sea life, and fishing has made Iceland a wealthy nation. In fact, 90 percent of Iceland's exports are fish or fish products.

But there is still plenty of fish and seafood for Icelanders to eat. It is common for Icelanders to eat fish or seafood at least once a day. In fact, in the past farm workers signed contracts stating that they had the right to refuse to be fed salmon more than once a day because they would become so tired of it.

Salmon, among other fish, live in Icelandic coastal

Smoked Salmon Spread

In the past, Icelanders smoked salmon as a way to preserve it. They still enjoy eating it today. Here is a recipe for smoked salmon spread.

Ingredients
8 ounces smoked salmon, chopped into small pieces
½ cup whipped cream cheese
½ cup plain Greek yogurt
2 green onions, finely chopped
1 teaspoon lemon juice
1 tablespoon chopped dill
salt and pepper to taste

Directions
1. Combine all the ingredients in a large bowl. Mix well.
2. Spread mixture on dark rye bread or crackers.

Serves 4.

Salmon spread is delicious and easy to prepare.

waters and in more than 100 of the nation's sparkling clean rivers. "Iceland," says Virginia chef Jeff Tunks, who buys much of the fish he serves from Iceland, "is the only place in the world where I'd drink from a stream."[2]

In the past, Icelanders dragged the rivers with nets. Because Iceland gets sunlight for about twenty hours daily in the summer, thousands of fish could be caught each day. Today salmon fishing is limited to six hours a day in order to protect the salmon population. In addition, salmon are grown in special, environmentally friendly tanks on fish farms. This is a big business in Iceland.

Salmon is not the only fish found in Icelandic waters and on Icelandic tables. Trout, halibut, herring, haddock, cod, and Atlantic char, a fish similar to salmon, thrive in Icelandic waters, too. Icelanders grill, fry, poach, bake, boil, dry, smoke, and salt these fish. They turn them into casseroles, fish balls, soups, and stews without wasting any part of the fish. Fish heads are used in soup, and cod cheeks and tongues are fried

Dulse is a crunchy, salty snack food made of dried seaweed.

or baked. An edible seaweed called **dulse** is dried and eaten as a snack. And, because of strict environmental laws, every bite is free of industrial pollutants and harmful chemicals.

Icelandic Lamb

Icelandic lamb, too, is pure and healthy. When the Vikings settled Iceland, they brought sheep, cattle, and horses with them. The cattle were reared for their milk, while the sheep were raised for wool, milk, and meat. Lamb was the most commonly eaten meat in Iceland. Even today, lamb remains extremely popular.

Icelandic cattle and sheep are **free range**. Rather than being kept penned up and fed man-made food,

Because they are raised free range, the meat of Icelandic lambs is lean, tender, and full of nutrients.

About Iceland

Iceland is part of Europe. It is a small country about the size of the U.S. state of Virginia. Its population is about 300,000. There are fifty-seven U.S. cities that have more people in them than the entire country of Iceland. It is a modern country with the highest literacy rate in the world. In Iceland, 100 percent of the people can read and write. No one in Iceland lives in poverty, and Icelanders have a long lifespan, ranking fourteenth in the world.

Iceland was ruled by Denmark until 1918. It is a democracy with an elected president and a parliament. Iceland's capital and largest city is Reykjavík (ray-kya-VICK). Much of the population lives in and around Reykjavík.

Despite its northern location, warm ocean currents keep Iceland from becoming extremely cold. The average yearly low temperature in Reykjavík is 35°F (1.9°F), and the average yearly high is 44°F (7°C). Winter lasts from September through April.

these animals are allowed to roam freely and to eat nutrient-rich grasses. The sheep are herded into the mountains in the summer, where they graze on a variety of wild plants. Because of Iceland's long summer days, the animals graze for more hours each day than they would in other locations. This makes them gain weight quickly so they can be slaughtered at six months rather than the more common age of eleven months. The meat of such young animals is leaner, sweeter, and more tender than that of older ones. "Icelandic lamb is

Skyr with Berries

Skyr is not easy to find in North America. It tastes a lot like Greek yogurt. This recipe uses Greek yogurt in place of skyr to make this popular Icelandic treat. Sugar can be used in place of honey. Add more sugar or honey for a sweeter taste.

Ingredients
2 cups plain Greek yogurt
1 tablespoon honey
1 cup blueberries

Directions
1. Mix all the yogurt and honey together.
2. Divide the yogurt mixture into two bowls. Top each with half the berries.
Serves 2.

Skyr is a nutritious sweet treat.

the best I've ever tasted," says Washington, D.C., chef Robert Wiedmaier. "It's very pure, nonfatty meat."[3] And, because the animals eat only nutrient-rich grasses, the meat, which Icelanders roast, grill, bake, boil, and smoke, is loaded with valuable minerals.

Dairy Products

Icelandic sheep are not raised only for their meat, however. The **ewes**, along with Icelandic cows, have provided Icelanders with milk, cream, butter, and cheese for over 1,000 years. In the past, most Icelanders kept at least one cow. Some of its milk was drunk or used in cooking. Some was made into cheese, a favorite Icelandic food. The rest was poured into pans and left out until the fatty part of the milk, the cream, rose to the top. It was then skimmed off and churned into rich butter, which Icelanders add to almost everything.

The remaining nonfat milk was used to make **skyr** (skeer), a soft, creamy cheese that looks and tastes like thick yogurt. "Essentially, skyr came about because of resourcefulness. After using the cream to make butter, the left-over non-fat milk was turned into skyr,"[4] explains Siggi, an Icelandic skyr maker.

Skyr is a typical part of the Icelandic people's diet. It is eaten in much the same way as yogurt—either plain or flavored with sugar, honey, or fruit, for snacks or light meals, in smoothies, or mixed in oatmeal. And, because it is fat free, high in protein, and contains no chemicals, skyr is nutritious.

Hearty Vegetables

Hearty vegetables are other healthy foods that Icelanders enjoy. Iceland has short summers and long, cold, dark winters, which makes it difficult to grow vegetables. In fact, there is no evidence of vegetables having been grown in Iceland until the middle of the 18th century. At that time, potatoes, rutabagas, and rhubarb were brought to Iceland from mainland Europe. These hearty vegetables thrived in Iceland's short summers,

Stalks of fresh-cut rhubarb are for sale at a local market.

could be stored or preserved easily for winter use, and soon became an important part of the Icelandic people's diet.

Today, Icelandic supermarkets overflow with imported vegetables. Vegetables are also grown in Icelandic greenhouses heated with **geothermal energy** piped in from Icelandic hot springs. Yet, even with many choices available, Icelanders still turn to their old favorites.

Potatoes, in particular, are extremely popular. "I know people who eat potatoes twice a day and would not consider a meal complete without them,"[5] explains Icelandic chef and author Nanna Rognvaldardottir. Icelanders boil potatoes and top them with sugar and butter. They also mash potatoes with butter and milk. Rutabagas, which are turnip-like vegetables with a sweet flavor and yellow flesh, are mashed in the same way. They are also added to soups and stews, and served with fish.

Rhubarb is used differently. Because the leaves are poisonous, only the plant's red stem is eaten. After boiling the rhubarb stem, Icelanders use it like fruit in jams, syrups, puddings, cakes, **tarts**, sweet soups, and **compotes**, which are sweetened stewed fruit. Rhubarb tastes pleasantly sour. It is also loaded with vitamins and minerals.

Like, rhubarb, the Icelandic people's favorite ingredients promote good health and taste delicious. Icelanders share a concern for the environment and the purity of their food, and they make sure that it is clean, flavorful, and wholesome. "The lambs eat the freshest grass; the cows drink the cleanest water; the fish swim in the purest seas," explains chef and Travel Channel host Andrew Zimmern. "Icelandic food tastes better because it is. Simple idea really."[6]

Chapter 2

Simple and Hearty

The Icelandic people's favorite dishes are simple and hearty. They do not need many spices but rather depend on fresh, local ingredients for flavor. Favorites include thick soups, poached and fried haddock, mashed fish, and roast lamb. These filling, flavorful, and nutritious dishes warm Icelanders on cold, dark days.

Thick, Warming Soups

Soup is a popular first course in Iceland. And, when it is served with dumplings or thick rye bread and sweet butter, soup is often a meal in itself. Halibut soup is among the favorites. Halibut is a large, mild-tasting white fish

A bowl of hearty lamb soup makes for a satisfying meal in Iceland.

that is so valued in Iceland that the Icelandic name for it means "holy fish."

Icelanders have been eating halibut soup for centuries. This sweet-and-sour dish is made with thick, fresh halibut steaks cooked in water with butter, lemon juice, prunes, sugar, and vinegar or **whey**. Whey is a milk by-product that forms when cheese is made. It has a sour taste. Icelanders include it to add tanginess to dishes.

The soup is ready when the fish is as soft as butter and the broth is loaded with flavor. Usually, the fish steaks are removed from the pot and served on separate plates with boiled potatoes. Bowls of broth are served on the side. Diners either cut up the fish and add it to the broth or eat the two separately. Some Icelanders add milk to the broth to make it creamy. Either way, the re-

Kjotsupa

This is a hearty lamb soup whose ingredients can vary. Cooks can add different vegetables depending on their taste. For more flavor, the meat can be browned before adding water. Water or broth, alone or together, can be used for the liquid. Spices can be added or removed to taste.

Ingredients
2 pounds lamb, cut into chunks
2 large carrots, peeled, cut in chunks
½ rutabaga (or turnip), peeled, cut in chunks
3 medium potatoes, peeled, cut in chunks
1 small onion, chopped
½ cup shredded cabbage
6 cups water
2 tablespoons rice
1 teaspoon garlic powder
1 teaspoon dried oregano
salt and pepper to taste

Directions
1. Put the lamb and rice in a large pot with the water. Bring to a boil.
2. Skim the fat off the top of the soup. Add the vegetables, spices, and salt and pepper to taste. Cover the pot. Cook on low for about 1 hour and 15 minutes. Stir occasionally and remove from the burner when the meat is cooked through and the vegetables are soft.

Serves 4.

sults are tangy, rich, and filling. Icelandic chef Volundur Snaer Volundarson recalls, "In my youth I quite often partook of this delicacy and remember distinctly how much I enjoyed it."[7]

Kjotsupa (kaht-SUH-pa), or lamb soup, is another Icelandic favorite. Every Icelandic cook has his or her own way of making it. According to Jo, an Icelandic cook and blogger, "There is a recipe for this soup in almost every Icelandic home. No two are the same and most are not really recipes but more like general guidelines. . . . The ingredients available will vary and so will the taste, mood, and inclination [desire] of the cook!"[8]

Typically, the soup is made with fresh local lamb and hearty root vegetables, like potatoes, carrots, rutabagas, and onions. Some cooks add rice or oatmeal to thicken it. Depending on how much water and thickener is used, kjotsupa can be a hearty soup or a dense stew. Both versions are quite filling and nutritious, which may be why it is a favorite among Icelandic athletes. Chef and television host Anthony Bourdain ate kjotsupa with a group of Icelandic weightlifters. They eat bowls of the soup before and after their workouts. They claim the soup gives them strength. According to Bourdain, "It's the kind of hearty peasanty food I really like. This heaping bowl of protein is the feed of choice for strong guys in training."[9]

Poached and Fried Haddock

Poached or pan-fried haddock are two other simple, healthy dishes that Icelanders enjoy. Haddock is a small

Poached haddock has a fresh, light taste.

Pan-Fried Fish

This is a popular Icelandic main course. It is often made with haddock, but any white fish will do. Flour and/or plain or seasoned breadcrumbs can be used to coat the fish. Seasoned breadcrumbs will make the fish taste a little spicier.

Ingredients
4 fish fillets, about ¼ pound each, skin removed
1 egg
⅔ cups flour or breadcrumbs
2 tablespoons milk
5 tablespoons butter
4 lemon wedges
salt and pepper to taste

Directions
1. Combine eggs and milk in a shallow bowl. Put breadcrumbs or flour in another shallow bowl. Add salt and pepper to taste.
2. Coat the fish by first dipping it into the egg mixture and then into the breadcrumbs.
3. Heat the butter in a large frying pan. Put the fish in the pan in a single layer. Cook the fish on medium heat until the bottom side is golden, about 3 minutes. Flip the fish and cook until the top is golden, about 3 more minutes.

Serve each piece of fish with a lemon wedge. Serves 4.

Pan-fried fish is tasty on its own, or dipped in ketchup or tartar sauce.

white fish related to cod. It is one of the best-loved fishes in Iceland. "Haddock," explains chef Nanna Rognvaldardottir, "is … what most Icelanders think of when they say 'fish.'"[10]

Poaching is a cooking process in which food is slowly simmered in liquids such as water, wine, milk, or broth. Icelanders poach fresh haddock steaks in water, seasoned with a sprinkle of lemon juice and a dash of pepper. Cooking fish in this manner helps keep it from drying out. The fish, which is usually served with boiled potatoes, is topped with fresh parsley or dill and a pat of butter. It has a fresh, moist, delicate

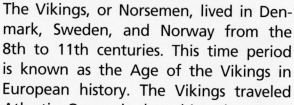

The Vikings

The Vikings, or Norsemen, lived in Denmark, Sweden, and Norway from the 8th to 11th centuries. This time period is known as the Age of the Vikings in European history. The Vikings traveled throughout the Atlantic Ocean in longships that were equipped with oars and sails. They traveled as far east as Constantinople, Turkey, and as far west as New Foundland, Canada. They raided many towns throughout Europe and built settlements in England, Ireland, and Europe. They colonized Iceland, Greenland, and Newfoundland, taking livestock and Irish slaves with them. Only the Viking colony in Iceland lasted. The Vikings described their lives in Iceland in an ancient writing form called runes. They also created myths and sagas, which were heroic tales about their adventures. These have been passed down in Iceland for generations.

taste that Icelanders love. In fact, in the past Icelanders usually ate poached haddock a few times a week. It still remains a favorite meal.

Pan-fried haddock is almost as popular. To make it, the fish is cut into pieces, rolled in flour or breadcrumbs, and lightly fried in butter. When the fish is crisp and buttery on the outside and tender and moist on the inside, it is served on a bed of mashed potatoes and topped with a slice of lemon. According to Volundarson, the dish "may seem simple … but I can assure you it is most splendid."[11]

Sea Bird Eggs

Icelanders eat sea bird eggs. The eggs are laid in the spring on outcroppings of steep cliffs located hundreds of feet above the ocean. Early Icelanders used ropes made of animal hide to get down the cliffs and gather the eggs. One man with a bag slung across his chest tied the end of the rope around his waist. Another man lowered him down. In order to reach the outcroppings, the climber used his feet to push himself from cliff to cliff in a swinging motion. When he filled his bag with eggs, he shouted for the watcher to pull him up.

Modern Icelanders still gather the eggs in much the same way. However, the man going down the cliff wears a helmet and safety harness attached to strong ropes and communicates with the man on top of the cliff with a walkie-talkie.

Mashed Fish

Icelanders are not wasteful people. Leftover poached haddock or any other leftover fish is not thrown away. Instead, it is mashed and turned into **plokkfiskur** (plok-FISS-kyer), which, according to an Icelandic blogger named Thoroddsson, "literally means mashed fish and that, not surprisingly is exactly what it is. Iceland when I was growing up was a place where fish was dirt cheap and, thus, a basic food and plokkfiskur was a standard way of dealing with fish leftovers. … [It was] one of my favorite dishes growing up."[12]

To make plokkfiskur, Icelandic cooks heat leftover fish and potatoes in white sauce, a velvety sauce made with milk, butter, and flour. Then, using a wooden spoon or a potato masher, they mash the whole thing into a coarse paste.

Plokkfiskur is usually served with a big hunk of dark rye bread spread with butter. Many people top the fish with butter, too. The result is a hearty, creamy, mild-tasting dish that is filling, healthy, and delicious. "Oh man that's good," Anthony Bourdain said upon tasting it. "This is what food should be."[13]

Sunday Roast

Roast leg of lamb is another dish that Icelanders enjoy. Icelandic families typically get together on Sunday for dinner, which is served in the afternoon. Roast leg of lamb has been the main course for centuries. The meat is lightly sprinkled with salt and pepper and roasted

Roast leg of lamb is typically the main course served at Sunday dinners in Iceland.

in the oven. The wild grasses and herbs that Icelandic lambs feed on enhance the flavor of the meat in much the same way as herbs and spices do, so little additional spice is needed.

New York food blogger Goldilocks explains:

> There is nothing more traditional than roast leg of lamb in Iceland. I worked on a vegetable farm for two summers in Northern Iceland and it was served almost every Sunday. . . . If you start out with fresh quality ingredients, simple preparations are always the way to go. This is true with this roasted leg of lamb; the only seasoning is freshly cracked pepper and kosher salt. No garlic, no thyme, no rosemary, and because this leg was grass-fed on our farm I think it is the best way to enjoy the complex but mild flavors.[14]

Thick, rich gravy made with pan drippings, butter, broth, and flour always accompanies the roast. Peas, rhubarb jam, rye bread, and sugar-glazed potatoes round out the meal. Sugar-glazed potatoes are very popular in Iceland. The Danes, people from Denmark who ruled Iceland for hundreds of years, brought the recipe to Iceland in the 19th century. The dish quickly became a national favorite. To make sugar-glazed potatoes, Icelanders boil potatoes. Then, they lightly fry them in melted sugar and butter. The sugar and butter form a candy-like coating on the potatoes, which adds a touch of sweetness and brightness to cold, dark Icelandic winter afternoons.

Indeed, delicious dishes like tender roasted lamb, moist and flaky poached haddock, crispy fried haddock, creamy plokkfiskur, tangy halibut soup, and thick, nutritious lamb soup fill and warm a person's stomach and spirit. No wonder they are among the Icelandic people's favorite foods.

Afternoon
Treats

Unlike countries in warmer climates, Iceland does not have lots of street vendors selling snack food to passers-by. It does, however, have many clean, modern coffee shops and bakeries where Icelanders can take an afternoon coffee break. Here, they enjoy coffee and different pastries or sandwiches while visiting with friends, reading the newspaper, or surfing the Internet. Icelanders also like to invite friends to afternoon coffee parties in their homes. At these parties an assortment of pastries and sandwiches is served.

Icelandic Doughnuts

Until the early 20th century, most Icelandic homes did not have an oven. Instead, Icelanders cooked in fire-

Kleinur are fried pastries that are typically enjoyed with a cup of coffee.

places in the home. Frying in pots held over the open flame was a popular way to make pastries. **Kleinur** (CLAY-ner), a deep-fried twisted pastry similar to a doughnut, has been eaten in Iceland for over 200 years and is still a popular accompaniment to afternoon coffee.

Kleinur is made with flour, sugar, butter, eggs, milk, and a hint of **cardamom**. Cardamom is an aromatic spice with a delicate taste similar to ginger. The Vikings brought it from Turkey to Norway and then to Iceland.

Kleinur takes skill to make. Forming the pastries into their usual twisted-bow shape is the first challenge. To form the pastries, cooks first cut the dough into diamonds. Next, they make a slit in the center of each diamond. Then they pull one end of the dough through the slit.

The pastries are then ready to be fried. Usually about six pastries are fried at the same time. In the past, Icelanders fried kleinur in sheep's fat. Today healthier vegetable oil is used. The oil must be just the right temperature—about 375ºF (191ºC). If it is not hot

Icelandic Names

Icelanders do not have family names that are passed down from one generation to another. Instead, Icelandic surnames, or last names, are taken from the father's first name. For example, if a Jon Stefansson has a son named Hans, Hans's full name will be Hans Jonsson, which means Hans, son of Jon. When Hans has a son that boy's surname will be Hansson. The same method is used for a daughter's last name. So, Jon Stefansson's daughter, Ingrid's, full name will be Ingrid Jonsdottir, which means Ingrid, daughter of Jon. Ingrid's name will not change when she marries. Icelandic women do not take their husband's name.

Culturally, surnames are not important in Iceland and Icelanders do not call each other by their surnames. They always use the other person's first name. Moreover, the Icelandic telephone book is organized alphabetically by first names rather than last names.

enough, the oil will make the pastries soggy. If it is too hot, the oil will burn them. Timing is also important. Cooks must be fast and alert. Kleinur is fried until the pastries are soft, puffy, and golden brown, which takes about two minutes. If they remain in the pot even a little too long, the pastries will not have the right texture. Because kleinur takes time and energy, Icelanders often make large amounts all at once. According to an Icelandic cook and blogger named Jo, "It is not unusual for a doughnut maker/housewife to make a double or even triple recipe in one session. . . . Making these delicacies is no small undertaking. It is time consuming and hard work, and therefore the batches are usually large to save time and effort."[15]

Most Icelanders would agree that the final result is worth the effort. Kleinur has a slightly sweet taste and a spicy aroma. Icelanders do not top the pastry with icing or powdered sugar. They like it plain with a steaming cup of coffee.

Paper-Thin Pancakes and Heart-Shaped Waffles

Ponnukokur (pon-noo-koo-KER), or pancakes, is another traditional Icelandic treat that goes well with coffee and does not require an oven. Ponnukokur has been a favorite Icelandic snack for centuries.

Icelandic pancakes are paper thin and incredibly light. They are more like delicate French crepes (crapes) than thick, fluffy American pancakes. Icelanders make them in a round skillet with a thick bottom. The thick

Thin Icelandic pancakes are quite different from typical American-style pancakes.

bottom keeps the pancakes from sticking to the pan or burning, which is essential since the pancakes are cooked over high heat.

Once the pancakes are hot and golden, they are sprinkled with lots of sugar and rolled into cylinders, or they are spread with rhubarb jam and whipped cream and folded into triangles.

The pancakes are served with coffee. "Almost everybody loves them and many will tell you that they consider ... this ... the most Icelandic dish there is,"[16] says chef Nanna Rognvaldardottir.

Like pancakes, waffles too are a popular afternoon

Waffles

You need a waffle iron to make waffles. The shape of the waffle depends on the waffle iron. This recipe uses a standard rectangular iron. For sweeter waffles add sugar.

Ingredients

2 cups flour
1½ cups milk
2 eggs
6 tablespoons applesauce
4 teaspoons baking powder
1 teaspoon vanilla
pinch of salt
nonstick cooking spray
strawberry jam to taste
whipped cream to taste

Directions

1. Combine the flour, milk, eggs, applesauce, baking powder, and salt. Mix well to form a batter.
2. Spray the waffle iron with the nonstick cooking spray. Heat the waffle iron.
3. Spoon the batter on the hot waffle iron. Cook until the waffle is golden brown. Repeat until all the batter is used up.
4. Put the waffles on individual plates. Top them with strawberry jam and whipped cream.

Makes about 8 waffles.
   Serves 4–8.

Icelandic waffles are usually made in a heart-shaped waffle iron.

snack. Icelandic waffles are usually made in a heart-shaped waffle iron. Such irons are used throughout Scandinavia and were brought to Iceland by the Danes, who had a big influence on Icelandic pastry making. The waffles are cooked until they are crisp on the outside and soft on the inside. Then, they are topped with sugar, rhubarb or berry jam, and a big spoonful of whipped cream. They are often served at coffee parties and are a delicious treat.

Beautiful Cakes

Once ovens were introduced to Iceland, Icelanders began baking in earnest. Delicious layer cakes, sheet cakes, and rolled cakes became very popular. Sold whole or by the slice in cafés and bakeries, cakes pair perfectly with afternoon coffee and are the center of attention at coffee parties. "All kinds of scrumptious decorated cakes with fruit, cream and/or sweet icing are very popular in Iceland. . . . These creations are as beautiful and tempting to behold as they are delicious and fattening,"[17] Jo explains.

Vinarterta (vin-er-TER-ta), which means Viennese cake, is a favorite choice. It is a layered pastry that originated in Vienna, Austria, and was brought to Iceland by the Danes. The cake has at least four layers held together with a paste made of boiled prunes, sugar, cinnamon, and cardamom. The dough for the layers is rolled out like piecrust, and is, in fact, more like thin pie dough than cake batter. Each layer of dough is baked in a separate pan. Then, each layer is spread with filling and stacked one atop the other. The cake is wrapped in foil or plastic wrap and stored in a cool place for a few days before it is eaten. During this time the flavors intensify and blend together. In fact, many Icelanders say that the cake tastes better the longer it is stored.

Spice Cake

Spice cake is a popular food to eat with coffee and is often served at coffee parties. It is mildly spicy and mildly sweet. Cardamom, allspice, or pumpkin pie spice can be added. For a more tart cake, plain yogurt can be substituted for vanilla yogurt.

Ingredients
2 cups flour
2 eggs
1 teaspoon baking soda
½ cup softened butter
⅔ cup sugar
1 cup vanilla yogurt
⅓ cup milk
½ cup raisins
½ cup walnuts or pecans (optional)
2 teaspoons cinnamon
1 teaspoon each ground ginger, nutmeg, cloves
½ teaspoon salt

Directions
1. Preheat the oven to 350°F. Spray a loaf pan with nonstick cooking spray.
2. Combine the sugar, butter, and eggs and mix well. Add the flour, spices, raisins, nuts, yogurt, and milk. Mix well.
3. Pour the batter into the loaf pan. Bake until a fork inserted in the center comes out clean, about one hour.
Makes one loaf. Serves 10–12.

The Land of Fire and Ice

Iceland is often called the land of fire and ice. Glaciers cover 10 percent of Iceland. Iceland also has a total of more than 200 volcanoes. Many of them are still active. The last major eruption occurred in 2010.

Iceland has vast lava fields, towering waterfalls, large hot springs in which Icelanders swim and soak, geysers, steam fields, long narrow inlets with steep sides called fjords (fee-ORDS), icebergs, green pastures, sea cliffs covered with puffins and other sea birds, mountains, rivers, and glacier lakes, where icebergs are calved, or break away, from glaciers.

From September through April, the aurora borealis, or the northern lights, is visible in Iceland's sky. It is a nightly display of dancing green, white, and red lights, similar to fireworks. The aurora borealis is caused by electrical activity in the outermost layer of the Earth's atmosphere.

Some Icelanders top the cake with whipped cream before serving it. Others serve it plain. Either way, according to cookbook editor Cheryl Long, "the vinarterta is very rich and incredibly delicious."[18]

Often each layer is a different color. One layer is left creamy white. Cocoa powder added to another layer turns it brown and gives it a chocolate flavor. Food coloring turns other layers pink and green. This type of vinarterta is called a rainbow cake. If the layers are flavored with cocoa powder and filled with rich buttercream instead of prune paste, the cake is known as a brown-striped cake.

Other popular cakes and pastries include mildly sweet spice cakes, cream layer cakes, fruit-filled layer cakes, rolled-honey cakes, chocolate cakes, tarts filled with rhubarb jam, and oatmeal bars and cookies.

Sandwich Cakes

Sandwich cakes are another popular afternoon snack. They are actually not cakes at all but are layered sandwiches decorated to look like cakes. Sandwich cakes are made by slicing a loaf of white bread lengthwise

Sandwich cakes are layers of bread spread with various fillings and "decorated" with tasty toppings.

into at least four parts. Each part becomes a layer that is spread with a filling. Some cakes contain only one type of filling, but most contain a different filling for each layer. Cooks make sure that the fillings go well with each other. Salmon and egg, tuna salad, egg salad, and shrimp salad are all popular fillings. The layers are held together with cream cheese or Icelandic mayonnaise, which looks and tastes like sour cream.

Mayonnaise or cream cheese is also used to "ice" the sandwich cake. The iced sandwiches are decorated with whatever the cook thinks will taste good with the different fillings. Parsley, hard-boiled eggs, pickles, bell pepper rings, cucumber rounds, carrot curls, tomato wedges, sliced canned peaches, grapes, tiny shrimp, and radish rosettes are all possibilities.

Indeed, Icelanders have lots of choices when it comes to their afternoon snack. Nibbles of sweet cakes, delicate pancakes, crispy heart-shaped waffles, soft twisted doughnuts, and savory sandwich cakes add to the fun of an afternoon coffee break or a larger coffee party.

4

Celebrating with Traditional Foods

Icelanders celebrate holidays with traditional food that is distinctly Icelandic. In fact, one important holiday, **Thorrablot** (thor-uh-BLOT), honors traditional Icelandic cooking. Historians believe Thorrablot started as a Viking celebration honoring the Norse god Thor. Over time, it has become a month-long, midwinter festival in which Icelanders attend banquets. At these banquets they celebrate their culture by feasting on traditional foods, singing old songs, and retelling Viking sagas.

Mashed Potatoes

Mashed potatoes is a popular Icelandic side dish, and is often served during Thorrablot and with Christmas dinner. Some Icelanders add a pinch of sugar to the potatoes.

Ingredients
4 medium potatoes, cleaned, peeled, cut into
   small chunks
⅓ cup warm milk
2 tablespoons melted butter
salt and pepper to taste

Directions
1. Put the potatoes in a large pot with enough cold water to cover them. Bring the water to a boil. Lower the heat. Cook until the potatoes are tender, about 15 minutes.
2. Drain the potatoes well. Put them in a large bowl. Mash the potatoes.
3. Warm the milk, so that it is hot but not boiling.
4. Add the milk, melted butter, salt, pepper, and sugar to taste. Mix well.

Serves 4.

A Part of History

Because Icelandic winters are long and dark, it has not always been easy for Icelanders to acquire food in the winter. To solve this problem, Icelanders traditionally spent much of the summer and fall gathering, preserving, and storing food to save for the cold months. Much of this food was pickled, dried, smoked, or **fermented** to keep it from spoiling. Fermented shark, dried fish, boiled sheep's head, and blood pudding were especially popular, and have since become Thorrablot favorites.

These traditional foods may seem strange to North Americans, but they are part of Icelandic history and culture. Chef Volundur Snaer Volundarson explains: "I am a great fan of the þorrablot [Thorrablot]. In the first place, I am very much in favor of keeping alive national traditions. Secondly, I thoroughly enjoy the opportunity to savor the foods served. It is always old-time traditional Icelandic food."[19]

Fish Specialties

Hákarl (HOW-karl), or fermented shark, is probably the most famous Thorrablot delicacy. The meat of the type of shark that lives in Icelandic waters is poisonous when fresh. But it is safe to eat once it ferments, or rots. To make it all right to eat, the meat is cut into long strips and buried in the earth, or placed in special enclosed boxes for two to four months. Then, it is hung to dry in the open air for at least another month. As the shark meat dries, the outside flesh hardens. Before the shark is eaten, the flesh is removed. The inner meat, which is cut into small cubes, is white and tender. It has a sharp taste and a powerful ammonia-like odor. Some people find the aroma unappetizing, but many Icelanders enjoy it. Volundarson says, "I like … the pungent taste and cleansing odor that fills the mouth and rises to the nostrils when a piece of shark is chewed,"[20] he says.

Harofiskur (har-o-FIS-ker), or dried fish, is another Thorrablot specialty. To make it, haddock or cod

Harofiskur, or dried fish, is made by drying cleaned, uncooked fish outdoors.

is cleaned then dried in the open air until it is brittle. Next, it is beaten with a mallet until it is soft. The uncooked fish, which is also a popular snack and travel food, is eaten plain or covered with butter.

Meat Specialties

A whole sheep's head is another Thorrablot treat. The head, which is served with the eyes and teeth showing, is not skinned. Instead, the wool is burnt off. Then, the head is split lengthwise; the brains are removed and stored in brine, or salted water, which preserves it.

Blood pudding is a type of sausage whose main ingredient is sheep's blood.

Traditionally, the head is boiled and served hot or cold with mashed potatoes or mashed rutabagas. It has a strong, hearty flavor, which many Icelanders love.

Blood pudding, too, has a strong flavor. Despite the name, it is not like the creamy dessert puddings that most Americans are familiar with. Blood pudding is instead a type of spongy sausage preserved with salt and spices. The main ingredient is sheep's blood, which is mixed with oats, rye flour, raisins, sheep's fat, salt, cinnamon, cloves, and dried **Iceland moss**, a plant with a salty flavor that grows on Icelandic cliffs and rocks. The mixture is boiled in a pouch made from the lining of a sheep's stomach. Once prepared, the pudding is left to cool. Before it is served, it is usually cut into slices and fried in butter. According to Travel Channel host Andrew Zimmern, "You can taste the blood. It's chewy. It is … like a dense cake. . . . This is delicious."[21]

Christmas Foods

Christmas is another important holiday in Iceland in which delicious, traditional foods are part of the celebration. Although there is not one specific menu that is served in every Icelandic home, a typical Christmas celebration is likely to include **ptarmigan** (TAR-mih-gihn) on Christmas Eve and smoked lamb on Christmas Day.

Ptarmigans are small, wild game birds that weigh about 1 pound (0.45kg) each. They have dark, dense meat that tastes more like beef liver than poultry. Hunting the birds has been a favorite sport in Iceland for centuries. To keep Iceland's ptarmigan population from shrinking, ptarmigan hunting is allowed only in November. During that month many Icelanders kill the birds, then hang, pluck, clean, and freeze them. Others buy ptarmigan in supermarkets the same way Americans buy chicken or turkey.

It takes about two birds to feed an average adult. The birds are stuffed with bacon, whose fat moistens them. Then they are browned in butter, covered with milk,

The ptarmigan is a wild game bird that is traditionally served on Christmas Eve.

and slowly simmered for about two hours. Before the birds are served, the milk is thickened with flour and cream and poured over the birds like gravy. The birds are usually served with sugar-glazed potatoes, rhubarb jam, peas, and cabbage.

Ptarmigan has a wild meaty flavor that Icelanders enjoy, especially on Christmas Eve. Indeed, according to chef Nanna Rognvaldardottir, ptarmigan is "so closely knit to Christmas that some people would be willing to

Christmas Leaf Bread

Laufabraud, or leaf bread, is special flat bread that Icelanders bake and eat for Christmas. Each slice of bread is a small work of art, decorated with a fancy cut-through pattern. Icelandic families often gather together in December to prepare leaf bread. The dough, which is made with flour, milk, sugar, and butter, must be rolled out until it is as thin as a sheet of paper. Then, it is cut into small circles. Using a knife or a cutting wheel, Icelanders cut snowflake-like designs into each circle. Just as no two snowflakes are exactly alike, neither are the designs on leaf bread circles. Once the circles are decorated, they are fried until golden brown.

The fried bread is wrapped in plastic and stored in a cool place until Christmas. Then the loaves are stacked on a platter and served with sweet soft butter.

Each circle of leaf bread can be as unique as the person making them.

postpone the festivities rather than miss it."[22]

Smoked Lamb

Smoked lamb is another Christmas favorite. It is eaten on Christmas Day in about 90 percent of Icelandic homes. In the past, Icelanders smoked lamb as a way to preserve the meat. Today Icelanders have freezers, making preserving meat unnecessary. Yet, they continue to smoke lamb because they like the taste.

The smoking process has not changed much since the Vikings brought it to Iceland. The meat is hung from the rafters in a shed or smokehouse, where a fire is kept burning in the middle of the room. The smokehouse has a small hole in the roof, which draws the smoke up to the rafters. There, it covers the meat, preserving it and giving it a rustic, smoky scent and flavor before it exits through the hole. The lamb is smoked for two weeks to a year. The meat that is smoked the longest has the strongest flavor.

The type of fuel used for the fire also affects the lamb's flavor. Dried sheep's dung, dried leaves, birch, willow, or juniper wood are all used as fuel. Dried sheep's dung is the most traditional choice, and is still a popular fuel. Icelanders like the earthy flavor it gives

Cabbage Apple Salad

Cabbage almost always is served with Christmas dinner. It may be cooked in vinegar and sugar, or it may be part of a salad. This is a popular Icelandic cabbage apple salad.

Ingredients
2 apples, washed and chopped
1 cup shredded cabbage
2 tablespoons canned pineapple, chopped and
   drained
½ cup sour cream or Greek yogurt
sugar to taste

Directions
1. Combine the cabbage and fruit in a bowl.
2. Add sour cream. Mix well. Add sugar to taste.
Serves 4.

Smoked lamb with red cabbage and potatoes is a Christmas dinner specialty.

off when burned.

The smoked meat is often sliced thin and eaten raw on dark rye bread, or wrapped around melon slices. For Christmas dinner, it is usually boiled and served with red cabbage and potatoes topped with white sauce. "I have fond memories of ... Christmas," explains Volundarson,

> We most often had smoked meat on the table and I can still feel the pleasant tingling in my nostrils as the aroma rising from the steaming pot of smoked meat filled the house. . . . It still happens that sometimes when my mind wanders back to my younger years, I find my mouth watering at the memory of my mother's smoked meat at holiday time.[23]

Special foods do indeed make holidays memorable. Although modern life in Iceland is much like that in the rest of the developed world, eating traditional foods on holidays helps Icelanders appreciate and remember their past and their culture. It also gives them fond memories of happy days.

Metric conversions

Mass (weight)

1 ounce (oz.)	= 28.0 grams (g)
8 ounces	= 227.0 grams
1 pound (lb.) or 16 ounces	= 0.45 kilograms (kg)
2.2 pounds	= 1.0 kilogram

Liquid Volume

1 teaspoon (tsp.)	= 5.0 milliliters (ml)
1 tablespoon (tbsp.)	= 15.0 milliliters
1 fluid ounce (oz.)	= 30.0 milliliters
1 cup (c.)	= 240 milliliters
1 pint (pt.)	= 480 milliliters
1 quart (qt.)	= 0.96 liters (l)
1 gallon (gal.)	= 3.84 liters

Pan Sizes

8- inch cake pan	= 20 x 4-centimeter cake pan
9-inch cake pan	= 23 x 3.5-centimeter cake pan
11 x 7-inch baking pan	= 28 x 18-centimeter baking pan
13 x 9-inch baking pan	= 32.5 x 23-centimeter baking pan
9 x 5-inch loaf pan	= 23 x 13-centimeter loaf pan
2-quart casserole	= 2-liter casserole

Temperature

212° F	= 100° C (boiling point of water)
225° F	= 110° C
250° F	= 120° C
275° F	= 135° C
300° F	= 150° C
325° F	= 160° C
350° F	= 180° C
375° F	= 190° C
400° F	= 200° C

Length

1/4 inch (in.)	= 0.6 centimeters (cm)
1/2 inch	= 1.25 centimeters
1 inch	= 2.5 centimeters

Notes

Chapter 1: Pure Healthy Food

1. "Home: Iceland: Wildlife: Fish," Iceland Worldwide. www.iww.is/pages/alife/fish/fish.html.

2. Quoted in Jen Murphy, "Should You Eat Like an Icelander?" *Food and Wine*, March 2010, p. 28.

3. Quoted in Murphy, "Should You Eat Like an Icelander?" p. 30.

4. Quoted in Adam Roberts, "Siggi's Skyr," The Amateur Gourmet, April 18, 2008. www.amateurgourmet.com/2008/04/siggis_skyr.html.

5. Nanna Rognvaldardottir. *Icelandic Food & Cookery*, New York: Hippocrene, 2002, p. 127.

6. Andrew Zimmern. *Bizarre Foods with Andrew Zimmern*, "How Do I Love Thee, Let Me Count the Ways," Travel Channel, March 11, 2008. http://blog.travelchannel.com/bizarre-foods/read/how-do-i-love-thee-let-me-count-the-ways/.

Chapter 2: Simple and Hearty

7. Volundur Snaer Volundarson. *Delicious Iceland*, Reykjavík, Iceland: Salka, 2006, p. 106.

8. Jo. "Soups, Stews, and Puddings," Jo's Icelandic Recipes. www.isholf.is/gullis/jo/Soups.htm.

9. Anthony Bourdain. "Strong Man's Soup," World Is Round. www.worldisround.com/articles/196986/text.html.

10. Rognvaldardottir. *Icelandic Food & Cookery*, p.64.

11. Voludur Snaer Volundarson. "Mother's Pan Sauteed Haddock," Icelandic Chef, November 13, 2008. http://icelandicchef.wordpress.com/2008/11/13/mother%e2%80%99s-pan-sauteed-haddock/.

12. Ari Thorrodsson. "Plokkfiskur," *Ari and His Food*, April 20, 2007. http://ariandhisfood.blogspot.com/2007/04/plokkfiskur.html.

13. *No Reservations: Iceland*. Season 1, Episode no. 3, first broadcast 1 August 2005 by The Travel Channel, Lydia Tenaglia, Executive Producer.

14. Goldilocks. "Icelandic Style Roast Leg of Lamb with Gravy," Food 52. www.food52.com/recipes/3845_icelandicstyle_roast_leg_of_lamb_with_gravy.

Chapter 3: Afternoon Treats

15. Jo. "Cakes, Pancakes, and Cookies," *Jo's Icelandic Recipes*. www.simnet.is/gullis/jo/Cakes_Pancakes.htm.

16. Rognvaldardottir. *Icelandic Food & Cookery*, p. 159.

17. Jo. "Cakes, Pancakes, and Cookies," *Jo's Icelandic Recipes*.

18. Cheryl Long, ed.. *The Best of Scan Fest*, Lake Oswego, OR: Culinary Arts, 1992, p.94.

Chapter 4: Celebrating with Traditional Food

19. Volundarson. *Delicious Iceland*, p. 198.

20. Volundarson. *Delicious Iceland*, p. 194.

21. *Bizarre Foods with Andrew Zimmern*, "Iceland," Season 2, Episode no. 2, first broadcast 11 March 2008 by The Travel Channel, Tacy Mangan, producer.

22. Rognvaldardottir. *Icelandic Food & Cookery*, p. 15.

23. Volundarson. *Delicious Iceland*, p. 175.

Glossary

cardamom: A spice similar to ginger.

compotes: Fruit desserts cooked in water and sugar.

dulse: A type of seaweed that is dried and eaten in Iceland.

ewes: Female sheep.

fermented: A chemical process in which sugar has been changed to alcohol, carbon dioxide, or organic acids. A method of preservation.

free range: The practice of allowing livestock to roam freely rather than keeping the animals in pens and stalls.

geothermal energy: Heat fueled by hot ground water.

hákarl: Fermented shark.

harofiskur: Dried fish.

Iceland moss: A green plant that grows on rocks and cliffs; it is dried and eaten.

kjotsupa: Thick lamb soup.

kleinur: A deep-fried twisted pastry.

plokkfiskur: Mashed fish and potatoes.

ponnukokur: Icelandic pancakes.

ptarmigan: A small game bird.

Scandinavia: Region of northern Europe that consists of Denmark, Sweden, Norway, Iceland, and Finland.

skyr: A soft creamy Icelandic cheese that looks and tastes like yogurt.

sustainable farming: Farming without harming the environment.

tarts: Little pies with an open top.

Thorrablot: Icelandic holiday that honors traditional Icelandic cooking.

Vikings: Early settlers of Iceland, also known as Norsemen.

whey: A milk by-product that forms when cheese is made.

For Further Exploration

Books

John James, *The Life and Times in the Viking World.* London: Kingfisher, 2007. This is an informative book about how the Vikings lived; included is a chapter on food.

Jennifer Miller, *Iceland.* Minneapolis: Lerner, 2010. Looks at Icelandic geography, landscape, culture, and people; with colorful photos.

Jonathan Wilcox, Zawiah Abdul Latif, *Iceland.* New York: Benchmark, 2007. This book focuses on Icelandic culture including, religion, daily life, and food.

Websites

Iceland.org (www.iceland.org). This is a site all about Iceland. The page for the Embassy of Iceland in Washington, D.C., offers a link to "Iceland for Kids," which has useful links and information about Iceland prepared especially for children.

KnowledgeBears.com "Iceland," (www.kbears.com/iceland/). A site for kids that offers information about Iceland with pictures, a map, statistics, a recording of the national anthem, and links.

Picturesofplaces.com "Iceland," (www.pictures ofplaces.com/Europe/iceland.html). Links to many pictures of Iceland, including its cities, volcanoes, steam fields, waterfalls, and icebergs.

Time for Kids "Iceland," (www.timeforkids.com/TFK /kids/hh/goplaces/main/0,28375,1018498,00.html). Aimed to help students with research writing and homework, this site has pictures, maps, information, timelines, and e-mail picture postcards.

Virtually Virtual Iceland (www.simnet.is/gardarj /gardar1.htm). This site contains lots of photos, Icelandic folktales, links to recipes, and much more.

Index

Picture credits

Cover Photo: photos.com/Shutterstock.com

© Andy Sutton/Alamy, 46

© Arco Images GmbH/Alamy, 10

© Arctic Images/Alamy, 47

© Bon Appetit/Alamy, 8, 21, 26, 50

© cm11/Shutterstock.com, 34

© C.O. Mercial/Alamy, 38

© Danita Delimont/Alamy, 6

© Darrin Jenkins/Alamy, 14

© Egill Gauti Thorkelsson/Alamy, 12

© Endantia/Alamy, 22

Gale, Cengage Learning, 5

© Gunnar Freyr Steinsson/Alamy, 33

© Icelandic Photo Agency/Alamy, 30

© JHB Photography/Alamy, 9

© Joe Gough/Shutterstock.com, 18

© Qrt/Alamy, 44

© Tommy Huynh/Alamy, 43

About the Author

Barbara Sheen is the author of more than 60 books for young people. She lives in New Mexico with her family. In her spare time, she likes to swim, walk, garden, and read. Of course, she loves to cook!